Grand Central Terminal

Phaidon Press Ltd
Regent's Wharf
All Saints Street
London N1 9PA

First published 1996

ISBN 0 7148 3346 0

A CIP catalogue record for this book is
available from the British Library.

Printed in Singapore

Grand Central Terminal
Warren and Wetmore

Kenneth Powell
ARCHITECTURE IN DETAIL

'One entered the city like a god,' Vincent Scully wrote famously of New York's Pennsylvania Station. 'One scuttles in now like a rat.'[1] The magnificent Penn Station, designed by the practice of McKim, Mead and White, was completed in 1910, and demolished in 1963 in the face of the first great preservation campaign to be waged in the United States. It was replaced by a new station which would be seen (the *New York Times* accurately predicted that same year) as an example of 'tin-can architecture in a tin-horn culture'.[2]

Penn Station has gone, but Grand Central survives, evidence that 'tin-horn culture' does not always triumph. One of a handful of structures which are universal symbols of New York, Grand Central Terminal stands at the true heart of Manhattan. It exemplifies the ideals and aspirations of a great American city consciously emerging as a world metropolis in the decade before the First World War. Without Grand Central, there would be no Rockefeller Center. The Terminal has, of course, shaped the destiny of Manhattan, but it is equally the foundation of a positive and optimistic urban philosophy which is one of New York's greatest contributions to twentieth-century life. Splendid and conspicuous as it is, Grand Central is more than a building: it is not just a civic monument, but the central component of a humane exercise in urban planning which set a new standard for New York and every other great city. Romantic, extravagant, gargantuan – overblown, even – as Grand Central seems to late twentieth-century sensibilities, it embodies a practical but progressive vision of urban life which has new relevance in the aftermath of the Modern Movement. Grand Central is nothing less than an urban dynamo powering the midtown area, which it transformed into the unchallengeable centre of Manhattan. The product of a free enterprise, profit-motivated system, it is the antithesis of the 'functional' and the utilitarian: Grand Central celebrates urban life as the new Penn Station degrades it. As the *New York Times* declared in 1913, its completion, soon after that of McKim, Mead and White's Pennsylvania Station, demonstrated that 'hard utilitarianism' had given way to a new vision of civic duty. The new stations were 'architectural monuments of a kind calculated to illustrate and to educate the aesthetic taste of a great Nation'.[3]

A century and a half ago, 42nd Street was anything but the heart of Manhattan. New York had grown out of the colonial settlement at the southern tip of Manhattan and the earliest railways were horse-drawn, connecting the commercial heart of the city with developing residential areas to the north. New York's first railway station was opened by the New York & Harlem Railroad in 1832 at Prince

4

1

2

3

1 Pennsylvania Station, New York City, completed in 1910 and demolished in 1963.
2 The concourse at Pennsylvania Station: exposed structural steel work used to supremely elegant effect.
3 The main waiting area at Pennsylvania Station was modelled on the great basilica and public baths of ancient Rome.
4 The entrance facade of Grand Central Terminal, on 42nd Street, is crowned by a colossal sculpture by Jules-Alexis Coutan.

Street, in the expanding warehouse district north of City Hall. The NY&H tracks ran along Fourth Avenue (as it then was) to the Harlem River. A few years later, through steam trains were introduced – an experiment which quickly proved unsuccessful when a locomotive blew up and steam power was banned from the city's streets. The NY&H steam railroad (incorporating the New Haven line which began a regular service to Boston in 1848) was pushed northwards, initially to a new terminal at Fourth Avenue and 26th Street, the site later to become Madison Square Garden. The Hudson River Railroad (Manhattan's second railroad, inaugurated in 1851) opened its station in 1861 at Tenth Avenue and 30th Street; 'not a very imposing structure', commented the press.[4]

Surface railroads were a cause of perennial complaint in New York. They were tolerated – at least until the emergence of the system of elevated railroads in the 1870s and 80s – but were equally seen as an obstruction to traffic and (if steam-powered) a potential fire hazard in a city with many surviving timber buildings and warehouses stuffed with flammable goods. Massive fires had ravaged large areas of the financial district in 1835 and 1845, obliterating many timber-framed buildings which remained from the era of Dutch administration. The city authorities quickly addressed the issue of fire by means of ordi-

nances banning steam locomotives south of 23rd Street firstly, and subsequently of 42nd Street in 1857, forcing the railroads to use horse traction south of this point. At 42nd Street, the New York Central Railroad, formed in 1853, established its transfer point and laid out sidings and sheds for steam locomotives and rolling stock. When the decision was taken to build a new 'Grand Central' terminal, this was the obvious site. Or so it seemed to Commodore Cornelius Vanderbilt, founder of one of the grandest of New York dynasties, that 'profane and scornful old parvenu' reckoned to be the richest man in the USA with an estate estimated at $90 million. The 'Commodore' had launched his career as a steamboat proprietor, with a ferry service between Staten Island and Manhattan, and became the railroad king when, in 1867, he merged the Hudson River Railroad with his newly acquired New York Central creating the dominant Railroad in the region, monopolizing traffic between New York, Canada and the booming Midwest metropolis of Chicago.[5] Not everyone shared Vanderbilt's faith in the Grand Central venture – to many, the location seemed peripheral, even remote, badly placed for the commercial heart of the city. It was, however, close to newly-fashionable residential streets; the Vanderbilt family itself was colonizing the area of Fifth Avenue below Central Park, spending (it was claimed) $15

5

6

7

8

5 View up Park Avenue, showing rail tracks in an open setting.
6 Interior of the first Grand Central Terminal, opened in October 1871.
7 The elaborately detailed exterior of Grand Central I, designed by John B Snook to conceal the great train shed.
8 Cartoon of Cornelius Vanderbilt, creator of Grand Central and the leading transport magnate of the age.

6

9 View down Park Avenue from Grand Central, shortly before the construction of the present terminal.
10 The construction of the new station involved massive demolition in the surrounding area.
11 The original terminal had an elegance and scale in keeping with the character of the newly-fashionable midtown area.

9

10

11

million on four houses, the finest of which was that designed by Richard Morris Hunt for William K Vanderbilt at the junction of 52nd Street.[6] Care was therefore taken to make the new Grand Central Terminal a structure of some architectural pretension. It cost over $6 million. John B Snook (1815–1901), a prolific architect whose commissions included many of the iron-fronted warehouses in SoHo as well as mansions for the elite, applied a rich dressing of eclectic Renaissance details which completely concealed the great train shed.[7] The latter was designed by the architects Robert Griffith Hatfield and Joseph Hatfield, who appear to have worked regularly with Daniel Badger's Architectural Iron Works, a vast factory located on East 14th Street which made many of the fine iron facades for the SoHo warehouse district.[8] With Isaac Buckhout as supervising engineer, the Grand Central shed took its cue from that of London's St Pancras Station – though it could not match the spectacular drama of the slightly larger London shed.

Opened in 1871, Grand Central I (the previous buildings on the site hardly constituted a passenger station) finally gave New York a rail terminus to compare with those in other great cities in the USA and abroad. Commodore Vanderbilt had been warned that the station would be 'the end of the world', but by the time it opened, the city was rapidly expanding

northwards and new transit connections (initially, the Third Avenue 'El' and later the IRT subway) were soon to provide an excellent link to the commercial downtown area; it was finally recognized that the business of getting people into the city was quite separate from that of transporting them around it. Grand Central I was itself an engine of urban growth, immediately attracting development to the midtown area. North of the terminal, the tracks ran in a wide cutting along the line of Park Avenue, potentially a development site of huge value, before entering a tunnel between 56th and 96th Streets.

The success of Grand Central I – the 'gateway to New York' as it soon became known – brought with it pressure for change. A substantial external remodelling in 1897–8 (with Bradford R Gilbert as architect and Walter Katte as engineer) toned down the exuberant frontages of the building in favour of a sombre classicism, and was quickly followed by another building campaign (with Samuel Huckel Jnr as architect) which concentrated on providing more comfortable amenities for passengers.[9] Between 1900 and 1910, passenger numbers on the New York Central Railroad rose by nearly 75 per cent; great as its freight traffic was, passenger traffic was an even bigger source of revenue. From its status as a wonder of the United States, Grand Central I was soon to be pilloried for being far too small for the traffic it had to serve. The 1900 reconstruction scheme did little to solve the inherent problems.

Not only was the terminal inadequate for its purpose – it was seen as an anachronism in a city of three and a half million people which was undergoing rapid change, and as part of a transport system out of tune with new perceptions of civic life; but also, in the era of the City Beautiful (ushered in by the success of the 1893 World's Columbian Exposition in Chicago) the smoke-filled yards of Park Avenue seemed a gross anomaly and an intrusion which should no longer be tolerated.

William J Wilgus (1865–1949), who became Chief Engineer of the New York Central in 1899, later recalled that 'the dangers and discomforts in the Park Avenue tunnel were calling aloud for abatement; the yard with its 575 trains a day, nearly three times the number that were handled in the 1870s, had become inadequate; the public was pressing for the restoration of cross streets and the abolition of the smoke nuisance at the yard…'.[10] Wilgus was convinced that further adaptation of the existing station, such as that carried out under his own supervision in 1900, was pointless. He was equally sure that a truly radical rebuilding, which addressed the problem of the Park Avenue yards and tunnel and enhanced the city, could be vastly profitable to the company.

Lacking formal education (having worked his way up from a menial position), but possessing great skills as a strategic planner as well as practical engineer, Buffalo-born Wilgus began to plan the electrification of the tracks into Grand Central as a first move towards the total reconstruction he advocated. In June 1901, the magazine *Railway Age* published Wilgus's draft scheme for a two-level Grand Central with electric suburban trains using a lower level terminal. There was some urgency in proceeding with such a plan, Wilgus argued, since 'the Board of Rapid Transit Commissioners of the city were intimating that they might by law secure the right to route their subway beneath the terminal, to the exclusion of such underground usage as the Railroad might find to be necessary…'.[11] With the 'Commodore' dead, the Vanderbilt influence on the New York Central had become far less decisive. Cornelius's son, W H Vanderbilt, died suddenly in 1885. His grandson, William Kissam Vanderbilt – a high-spending socialite whose daughter was to marry the Duke of Marlborough – was the last member of the family to be active in its management and served as its Chairman for some years. Wilgus's proposals received a depressingly apathetic response from the Railroad's board. Their apathy was soon shaken. In January 1902, two suburban trains collided in the Park Avenue tunnel: 15 people

12

13

12 The 1893 Columbian Exposition in Chicago provided a vivid illustration of the potential of monumental classicism and was a symbol of the 'American Renaissance'.

13 The partial reconstruction of Grand Central in 1897–8 reflected the new classical taste, though with somewhat ponderous results.

14 The rebuilding of Grand Central involved massive changes to the Manhattan Street scene.

15 View of the construction site in 1911, with St Patrick's Cathedral in the background.

14

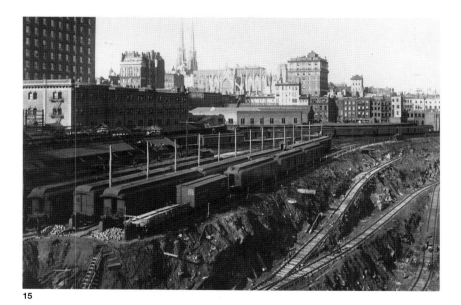

15

were killed and many more injured. Bad visibility caused by smoke was blamed for the tragedy. There was an outcry, with the Railroad accused of criminal negligence. The following year, a New York State act banned all steam traction south of the Harlem River – the New York Central and the New York, New Haven & Hartford Railroad (which also used Grand Central) were given five years to implement the order. An agreement with the city authorities, which laid down what became the framework for rebuilding Grand Central as an all-electric terminus, closely reflected Wilgus's earlier proposals. Eleven cross streets (45th to 55th) were to be reinstated above the tracks. Park Avenue, which then ended at 49th Street, was to be extended southwards. The Terminal, in short, was to be integrated into the city.

Initially, it was believed that this could be achieved by a radical adaptation of the existing building. Wilgus doubted that this was the best course, envisaging instead 'a double-level under-surface terminal on which to superimpose office quarters and revenue-producing structures made possible by the intended use of electric motive power'.[12] Wilgus created a vice-president of the Railroad in 1903) believed that the utilization of air rights was the key to a project which he had nurtured for several years. Electric trains did not require lofty train sheds or open air. 'Thus from the air would be taken wealth with which to finance obligatory vast changes otherwise non-productive. Obviously it was the thing to do', he argued.[13] Wilgus's arguments eventually convinced the New York Central board, clearly reluctant to scrap a building which had been expensively updated within the last few years, and to commit an estimated $43 million to rebuilding plans which were eventually to cost nearly twice that sum.

The first electric train into Grand Central ran on 30 September 1906 – a photograph taken that day shows the purposeful modern machine looking slightly incongruous against the ornate background of the 1871 shed. New Year's Eve of 1906 saw the departure of the last steam train from the old, doomed terminal. The construction of the new terminal building was not yet begun, but the much bigger process of urban reconstruction, of which it formed part, was already well underway.[13] The clearance of a wide swathe of land between Madison and Lexington Avenues – 200 buildings were demolished – began in 1903 and the first of the air rights buildings was completed by 1908. Six more were complete before the new terminal opened. Into the vast excavations went the two layers of tracks required by the Wilgus plan, those at the upper level being laid on concrete slabs resting on huge steel girders. The great engineering operation was carefully phased to allow trains to operate throughout.

The Wilgus 'master plan' provided a framework within which an architect could be sought for the terminal itself. By 1903, the year that an 'informal' competition was held, New York was in the midst of a massive building campaign which produced some of the city's best-known public monuments – the Metropolitan Museum, Public Library and US Customs House, for example – as well as an unprecedented wave of new commercial development.[14] The predominant architectural style of the age – that of the 'American Renaissance' – was a rich and eclectic classicism. Charles McKim of McKim, Mead and White, the most famous practice of the period, wrote of his method of working: 'by conscientious study of the best examples of classic periods, including those of antiquity, it is possible to conceive a perfect result suggestive of a particular period but inspired by the study of them all.'[15] McKim had scored a coup in 1902 by winning the commission to design a vast new station in Manhattan for the Pennsylvania Railroad, the New York Central's great competitor which had previously terminated on the New Jersey side of the Hudson River at the notorious Manhattan Transfer Station. The firm, this time represented by Stanford White, was invited to submit proposals for the new Grand Central – a project which must have seemed all the more urgent in view of the threat from the 'Pennsy'. Also on the invited

shortlist were the prestigious Daniel Burnham and Company of Chicago (masterplanners of the 1893 Columbian Exposition, their Union Station, Washington DC, was begun in 1903). The two other competitors were established consultants to the New York Central – Samuel Huckel (Wilgus's past collaborator) and Reed and Stem of St Paul, who specialized in railway stations and worked for a number of railroad companies.[16]

McKim, Mead and White produced a striking proposal which, in a strange premonition of the 1960s placed a skyscraper office tower – it would have been the tallest in the world – above the Terminal. The Terminal building would have been penetrated by arcaded streets, allowing the city's traffic to flow through it. However, the competition was won by Reed and Stem. Charles Reed was, in fact, Wilgus's brother-in-law and it seems possible that he benefited from Wilgus's advice on their entry. The firm's winning proposal certainly accorded closely with Wilgus's planning concepts, giving them a striking architectural expression. The elevated terminal building was to be surrounded by a wide roadway which took traffic around rather than through it. Inside the building, stairs were to be avoided in favour of ramps. Both concepts were crucial to the building as completed. However, Reed and Stem's proposal for a grandiose 'Court of Honour',

16

17

16 Main elevation of the Terminal as built, but showing the unexecuted office department over part of the site.
17 The 'Court of Honour' proposed by competition-winners Reed and Stem was never constructed.

10

18

19

20

with magnificent classical buildings including a new opera house surrounding a vast square along Park Avenue North, was never taken up, although it provided an optimistic blueprint for the air rights development along the Avenue. Reed and Stem gave New York its clearest vision to date of the City Beautiful.

Reed and Stem may have been declared competition winners, but they were to be robbed of the chance to build the new Grand Central to their competition designs. Although the Vanderbilts were no longer major shareholders in the New York Central, their influence was still considerable. William K Vanderbilt, Chairman of the board, was unhappy with the appointment of Reed and Stem and proceeded to invite another practice, Warren and Wetmore, to act as their collaborators.

According to Wilgus, Warren and Wetmore had challenged the competition outcome as soon as it was announced, offering an alternative plan that was 'unworkable'. Having failed, they resorted to 'social influence'.[17] Whitney Warren (1864–1943) was, in fact, Vanderbilt's cousin. Born to inherited wealth, he went to Paris to study at the Ecole des Beaux-Arts at the age of 20. He remained in France for ten years, becoming ardently Francophile in all matters, not least that of architectural style. One of his first significant jobs following his return to the

USA was to design a country house for another wealthy young man, Charles Wetmore. Wetmore (1866–1941) had trained as a lawyer, but was passionately interested in architecture and is said to have designed three university dormitories while still at Harvard Law School. The two became friends and professional partners, Wetmore undertaking formal architectural training after the launch of the firm of Warren and Wetmore in 1898. The practice appears to have been dissolved in the early 1930s with the retirement of the two principals.[18]

Warren and Wetmore were highly successful not just in New York, where they designed most of the air rights blocks around Grand Central as well as private mansions, commercial buildings and even the delightfully nautical New York Yacht Club on West 44th Street, but throughout the USA and abroad. From Grand Central, they went on to design stations at Detroit and Kansas City and to plan a massive terminal in Moscow. Hotels were another speciality and the firm found clients in Canada, Cuba, Puerto Rico and even China. One of their more unusual commissions was the reconstruction of the University Library at Louvain, Belgium. Warren was, significantly, a member of the commission established by the city in 1904 to draw up a masterplan for a programme of radical civic improvements in New York, and Vanderbilt's decision to include his practice in the design team may reflect public pressure for a station truly worthy of the city. A letter from the Fine Arts Federation of New York published in the *New York Times* in March 1903, declared that the new station should be 'a monument and an ornament to the city'. When the commission's report was finally published in 1907, it contained surprisingly little of substance on the matter of transportation.

Wilgus later commented on the appointment of Warren and Wetmore that they created 'turmoil'. The intruders, he continued, 'applied the epithet of "grocery store plan" to what had been done, and sought to change the design to one more monumental in character, devoted solely to railway purposes'.[19] Sympathetic as he was to Reed and Stem, Wilgus conceded that 'the warring views in the end resulted in compromises that in some ways were praiseworthy'. However, he deplored Warren and Wetmore's suggestion – taken up for a time by the client – that the elevated roadways around the building be omitted; they were, in fact, later reinstated. A later proposal by Warren, always a strict exponent of the Beaux-Arts, that the innovative ramp system should also be abandoned was quashed at the insistence of the New Haven company, normally a quiescent tenant of the New York Central.[20]

The relationship between the two 'collaborating' practices (who worked together under the title 'Associated Architects of Grand Central Terminal') was never especially cordial. Charles Reed died in 1911, while the new Terminal was under construction, and Warren and Wetmore were quickly appointed sole architects at the suggestion of the canny Wetmore. Stem, not unnaturally, went to law and, after years of litigation, won his case in 1920 and got $500,000 in damages and costs. The judgment led to Warren's expulsion from the American Institute of Architects on the grounds of unprofessional conduct.

William Wilgus left the New York Central in 1907, his strikingly successful career with the Railroad blighted by another tragedy. In February of that year, one of the company's new electric trains came off the rails – 25 people were killed after the cars of the train caught fire. A broken rail was blamed. There was talk of arresting the entire Railroad board, but New York Central President, William H Newman, appeared to hold Wilgus solely responsible and the latter faced possible indictment for manslaughter. Wilgus was subsequently exonerated – the accident was blamed on excessive speed – but he resigned and went into private practice, a move that he had, been considering for some time, he later claimed.[21] The massive Grand Central project was no more than 40 per cent complete at the time and his resignation was a clear setback. It was reported in the press that W K Vanderbilt, 'the directing head of the

21

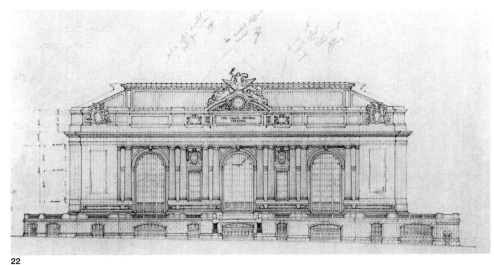

22

23

system … is now in France racing horses and has been there for several months. He is paying practically no attention to the road…'.[22]

Between 1903 and 1907, 73 contracts were let for the construction of the new Terminal and yard.[23] The project involved more or less complete reconstruction of an entire city district – 25 miles of sewers had to be moved or replaced. Buildings which adjoined the huge site had to be underpinned. The station itself had grown since the first plans were approved in 1903. Then 43 tracks had been planned, but 67 were eventually constructed – more than were ever really required. Everything about the new Terminal was on a huge scale, designed to handle three times the traffic of its predecessor.

The architectural form of the Terminal as finally built represents a radical break with Reed and Stem's competition-winning scheme. Their proposal for a 23-storey hotel on adjacent land was dropped, as was the idea of a 'Court of Honour', and the terminal building itself completely redesigned. But Warren and Wetmore's competition scheme was similarly discarded, and by the end of 1904, an entirely new, effectively composite, design had emerged. Taking its cue from contemporary Paris, the revised scheme was distinguished by a vast steel and glass roof – like that of the Grand Palais built for the 1900 Paris Exhibition – clearly expressed on the exterior. By 1907, a further process of redesign had been completed and the high vault had been abandoned. The main elevation of the Terminal, dominated by three great arched window openings – a triumphal arch for a city gateway – was, in essence, that finally built, though the elevated roadway system had yet to be reinstated. Construction did not begin until 1910 – the last train left the old terminal on 5 June of that year – by which time Warren and Wetmore appeared to have achieved a dominant role in the design process. If one decisive hand was apparent in the final designs, it was that of Whitney Warren. William Wilgus had provided evidence for Allen Stem when the latter took to law to assert his practice's rights in the Grand Central commission; the detailed account he drew up at that time may have formed the basis for Wilgus's authoritative paper, written towards the end of his life, on 'The Grand Central Terminal in Perspective'. However, Wilgus conceded that the 'intrusion' of Warren and Wetmore had some positive consequences. Warren's strong grounding in the architecture of the Beaux-Arts was critical in the final designs for the elevational treatment of the terminal, which date from 1910. During 1909–10, a collaborative scheme for the building, faithful to Wilgus's initial ideas and reflecting the contribution of both the architectural practices involved, emerged and was subsequently constructed, with some variations, from 1911–13.

24

24 The newly completed
facade of the Terminal on
42nd Street, before the
great sculptural centre-
piece was installed.
25 Coutan's large sculp-
ture was finally hauled into
position between March
and July 1914.
26 The figure of Minerva
symbolized the wisdom of
the Terminal's builders.

25

15

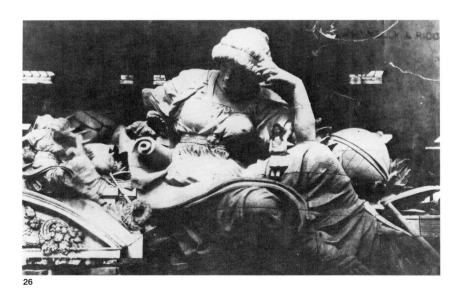

26

If there was a model for the new Terminal (and it was one that Wilgus freely acknowledged), it was the Gare d'Orsay in Paris, designed by Victor Laloux and opened in 1900. Significantly, the Gare d'Orsay (which now houses the Musée d'Orsay) was designed for all-electric operation, so that the platforms and waiting areas could be combined under one roof – travellers descended broad staircases from the main concourse to board their trains. Earlier versions of the Grand Central project showed a similar arrangement – a 'train room' integrated into the concourse with the upper level of platforms clearly visible from the waiting areas. As constructed, the platforms were depressed slightly below the level of the main, express concourse, 'the finest big room in New York', as *Architectural Forum* described it in 1954, which itself sunk below street level. A similar arrangement applies at the lower, suburban concourse level – it is possible to walk through Grand Central without ever being conscious of the presence of trains.

Grand Central Terminal was consciously designed to dominate midtown Manhattan. Ironically, the huge amount of development which the Terminal quickly generated resulted in its being obscured by a mass of new building. Only from the south, up Park Avenue, is there now a distant view of the building (albeit overshadowed by the bulk of the former PanAm tower). On 42nd Street, however, the terminal is still a formidable presence, a symbol of America's new industrial and cultural might, fusing modern building technology with fine traditional materials. Grand Central was, of course, the prime public expression of an engineering operation which had extended over a decade. The steel frame on which it rose was not innovative – steel-framing had come to New York in the 1880s – but it was extremely complex, with main columns driven right down into the bedrock. The task of the engineers (working under Wilgus's successor at the New York Central, George Kittredge) was made all the more difficult by the lack of a clear correlation between the layout of the tracks and the terminal itself, imposed, as it were, arbitrarily on the rail pattern below. In typically Beaux-Arts fashion, the architects made no attempt to express the frame, which confidently supported a heavy cladding of Indiana limestone and Connecticut granite.

Warren's massive arched facade on 42nd Street impresses not just by its sheer scale, but equally by its relative starkness. Ornament is used sparingly but with exuberant boldness, culminating in the huge and effusive sculptural group (weighing 1,500 tons) representing 'The Glory of Commerce', designed by the Parisian sculptor Jules-Alexis Coutan who had worked on the new Hôtel de Ville and Opéra

Comique in Paris. Executed in the USA it was craned into position in July 1914, to mark the final completion of the terminal. Other sculptural work was entrusted to another Parisian sculptor, Sylvain Salières, who worked in an equally conservative manner.[24] Both these artists were appointed at the behest of Whitney Warren. Ever the faithful son of the Beaux-Arts, Warren subjugated decoration to the overall unity of the design – there was no scope for the imaginative commissioning policy pursued, two decades later, by the builders of the Rockefeller Center. Grand Central has an austerity which appeals to modern sensibilities. At Penn Central, McKim, Mead and White created an elaborate and lavish evocation of Roman glories. The architects of Grand Central pursued a more progressive, astylar aesthetic.

Grand Central was designed to handle both a huge commuter traffic and a highly-profitable long-distance railroad. The New York Central's legendary *20th Century Limited* made its first run in 1902, reaching Chicago in 20 hours; by 1947, the journey time had been cut to 15 hours. There were other famous trains – the *Empire State Express* (New York–Detroit), the *Ohio State Limited*, the *Pacemaker* and, by the 1940s, a through sleeping-car service to Los Angeles – all of which succumbed to the rise of air travel in the 1950s and 60s.[25] Grand Central is now exclusively a commuter station,

but its form reflects a clear demarcation between its two distinct functions. The idea of a two-level station was, of course, that of William Wilgus and was effectively incorporated into the final designs. Long-distance travellers use the magnificent main concourse, 470 feet long and 160 feet wide, floored in Tennessee marble and lined (above an Italian marble dado) with simulated Caen stone. Recent research indicates that the latter material is actually precast plaster, attached to an infill of hollow clay blocks.

The main concourse remains perhaps the greatest room in New York, a masterpiece of Beaux-Arts design. The great flight of steps which descends from Vanderbilt Avenue has echoes of Garnier's Paris Opéra, completed in 1875 and well-known to Warren. A similar arrangement was intended on the west side of the concourse but, for reasons unknown, was never constructed. The concourse contained the ticket booths, information desk and baggage check-in, all beneath a vast painted ceiling designed by the artist Paul Helleu – a fashionable portraitist who had painted W K Vanderbilt's daughter, Consuela.[26]

Helleu's scheme was actually executed by Charles Bassing of Brooklyn, who may have been responsible for reversing the proper order of the constellations of the winter and spring sky – a blunder quickly noticed by an observant commuter. The frescos were painted directly onto the plaster of the

27

27 The central figure of Mercury was a symbol of communications; although, ironically, the god was also the patron of thieves and vagabonds. The flanking figures of Minerva and Hercules symbolized, respectively, mental and physical energy.
28 The first stone was set in place in July 1914 – recorded in this picture given by Whitney Warren to the millionaire philanthropist J Pierpont Morgan.

29 A view of the main concourse in 1931 – a model of civilized and efficient urban building.
30 View of Grand Central Terminal c1930, with the Commodore Hotel to the right and the New York Central Office Building in the background.

29

30

ceiling, the stars picked out with gold leaf and illuminated by hundreds of electric bulbs. However, the decorative scheme had deteriorated so badly by the 1940s as a result of water penetration that it was redone on asbestos panels.[27]

An earlier proposal, for a barrel-vaulted roof pierced by a large area of glazing, appears to have been quickly rejected.[28] This arrangement would have considerably increased the level of natural light in the concourse area, but equally would have created problems with solar gain on hot Manhattan summer days. For over 80 years, Grand Central has offered a well-tempered internal environment, thanks to an effective system of natural ventilation. Only now is some form of assisted ventilation being contemplated.

The aim of the architects was to make a building which elevated the idea of urban life. Thus the finest spaces at Grand Central were for people, not trains, and excelled anything seen in recent European termini. Broad galleries on three sides provided a place to stroll and watch the animated scene below. While McKim, Mead and White's great glazed concourse at the Pennsylvania Station was matched by a waiting room of similar proportions (clearly modelled on the Baths of Caracalla), Grand Central's architects made the concourse the clear focus of the building. The long-distance waiting room was an adjunct,

though large in scale and comfortably furnished. Dominated by huge electroliers of gilt metal, it provided a refuge for departing passengers more conventional in form than the other interiors at Grand Central.

'Clarity, directness and simplicity' were, according to Carroll Meeks, the characteristics which set Grand Central apart from the other great stations of the age.[29] The determination of the architects to avoid any of the confusion and crowding found at other big city stations produced the Incoming Station, with its own concourse, west of the express concourse. Opened in 1914, together with the Biltmore Hotel in which it was incorporated, this space was later reduced in height when the Biltmore's own lobby was expanded, but it remained possible for arriving passengers to pass through Grand Central without ever encountering the express concourse. The thinking behind this arrangement was novel in terms of contemporary station design and looked forward to the airports of the late twentieth century.

Reed and Stem's ramp system is an equally progressive device which, though at odds with conventional Beaux-Arts thinking, is a vital component in the mechanics of Grand Central. The broad ramps (obscured in recent years by makeshift offices) which dive down to the former suburban concourse, continue the line of a ramped route from the street.

31, 32 The majestic, light-filled concourse is one of the greatest of American interiors, 'the gigantic stage on which are played a thousand dramas daily'.

The suburban concourse originally duplicated all the amenities – ticketing, baggage and information – found above, while the Terminal's main restaurant (now the Oyster Bar) was located at an intermediate level. Inside the Oyster Bar, the vaulting system of Guastavino tiles is clearly visible. The Guastavino system acquired a certain vogue in early twentieth-century New York, being employed, for example, at the Cathedral of St John the Divine.[30] Whereas McKim's Pennsylvania Station featured consider-able areas of exposed steelwork, the colossal steel frame of Grand Central was carefully concealed beneath masonry facings – only when the platforms are reached is the structural skeleton of the building apparent. After the calm of the terminal above, the relative modesty of the platforms may come as a surprise. But, as Carl Condit points out, 'this gigan-tic walled temenos … possesses an awesome, infernal character that stands in profound contrast to the high-style splendors and costly materials of the head-house'.[31] Electric locomotives did not require lofty spaces and the 71 acres of tracks beneath Grand Central have something of the char-acter of contemporary subway stations; they were functional spaces, not intended for anything beyond the process of boarding or descending from trains. Although Grand Central has always been a terminal – unlike Penn Station – the complications of revers-ing out every train were alleviated in the rebuilding by means of through loops of track at both levels. They remain, but are no longer used by the com-muter trains of today. Even as the new Terminal was being constructed, New York's subway system was growing and provision had to be made for integrat-ing it into the project – at one stage, as many as seven levels of rail tracks were envisaged. 'The greatest multi-level transit nexus ever conceived', as Condit describes it, never materialized in this form, but the new Grand Central efficiently inte-grated links to a major subway interchange as well as a pedestrian circulation system servicing the vast air rights development above.[32]

The 'Grand Central Zone' occupying an area of Manhattan between Lexington and Madison Avenues, extending from 42nd Street to 51st Street, was, William Wilgus proudly wrote towards the end of his life, 'a self-contained city clearly evident to the casual onlooker who little knows that beneath it are the terminal yards…'.[33] The air rights development had got underway before the completion of the Ter-minal itself, but the world crisis of the First World War, and the temporary economic depression which struck America after the armistice, slowed its progress. The first eight blocks to be developed were concentrated along Vanderbilt Avenue and Lexington Avenue and included: the Biltmore Hotel

33, 34 The ceiling of the concourse was decorated with a vast painting by Paul Helleu showing the constellations. Executed soon after the opening of the station, it began to deteriorate within a few years and was redone on asbestos panels in the 1940s. These photographs show the ceiling painted in an unfinished state.

35

35 The restaurant – later known as the Oyster Bar – was located between the express and suburban concourses. It is vaulted in Guastavino tiles.

36 The main waiting room (recently restored) is a magnificently assured space in the most expansive classical manner. The splendid light fittings survive today.

35

36

(between Vanderbilt and Madison Avenues at 43rd to 44th Streets) designed by the architects of the Terminal and opened in 1914; James Gamble Rogers's Yale Club (1915), convenient for trains to New Haven; and the Post Office Building east of the Terminal. Subsequently, a series of apartment buildings rose along Park Avenue, a thoroughfare which the Railroad had created, albeit by chance. The grandest of these buildings, the Marquery, was designed by Warren and Wetmore and opened in 1918. The Hotel Commodore, also by Warren and Wetmore, opened in 1919 on a site flanking the principal 42nd Street frontage of the station. With 2,000 rooms and a function room which could contain 3,500 guests, it was one of the largest hotels of the age and certainly the biggest in New York. It survives, but has been radically recast and covered in bland curtain walling as the Grand Hyatt.

Only in the mid-1920s were further buildings completed, but by 1931 all the available air rights space had been taken up by further hotels, the last of them being Schultze and Weaver's magnificent Waldorf Astoria boasting its own private rail siding, and office buildings. The continuing, and ever more intense, pressure for development in midtown Manhattan was reflected in the vast bulk of the Graybar Building at 420 Lexington Avenue by architects Sloan and Robertson, completed in 1927 and

replacing an earlier air rights block. The Graybar was joined to the terminal by a lofty vaulted passageway, featuring murals by Edward Trumball (1882–1969), and was a logical and finely executed extension of Grand Central's circulatory system and a clear premonition of the progressive urbanism of the Rockefeller Center. The New York Central Building was built in 1928–30 to designs by Warren and Wetmore and intended as a grand end-stop to Park Avenue from the north. Tacked on to the large, relatively plain Railroad office building, its exuberant, ornate decoration harked back to earlier Manhattan skyscrapers like the Singer and Woolworth and was out of tune with the Deco spirit of the Chrysler and Empire State towers, completed in 1930 and 1931 respectively. (The Chrysler was, of course, close to Grand Central, a product of the midtown boom.) Imposing as the New York Central (latterly Helmsley) Building is, it suggested that Warren and Wetmore had lost their touch; indeed, the firm built little after 1930. The construction of the building provided the impetus for the belated completion of the upper-level road around the entire Terminal, the 'circumferential plaza' that was a vital element in Reed & Stem's original, competition-winning scheme of 1903. With the air rights development complete, an annual income of $4 million was guaranteed to the Railroad. The terminal itself had, inevitably, sunk into the variegated clump of towers which it had generated. Yet the area around Grand Central was as architecturally rich and varied as any in Manhattan – there was even a church, St Bartholomew's, designed by Bertram Goodhue. It was truly 'a city within a city'.

By 1945, Grand Central was handling 600 trains and 180,000 passengers on a typical working day. One summer day in 1947 a record quarter of a million people arrived or departed from the Terminal; the next year saw a five per cent decline in passengers, a trend which gained momentum in the next few years. Not until the mid-1950s, however, did air travel begin to attract large numbers of long-distance passengers away from the trains. It was in 1953 that the long-running radio serial, 'Grand Central Station', launched in 1937, was axed – its images of the terminal as the 'crossroads of a million private lives … Gigantic stage on which are played a thousand dramas daily' remain familiar 40 years later. Grand Central featured in film and literature, a symbol both of the splendours and, more recently, the terrors of the city.

The reality of Grand Central had entirely fulfilled the vision which William Wilgus had offered at the turn of the century, producing huge rentals for the Railroad and genuine civic improvements, as well as providing efficient facilities for travellers. But the serious decline of passenger revenues in the 1950s cast doubt on the commercial viability of the Terminal. At

first, its owners looked at ways in which it could be run more cost-effectively – parts of the building were closed at night, automated ticket machines reduced staff costs and advertising spaces were let. In 1950, Kodak erected its notorious hoarding on the east gallery of the main concourse – in time, this developed into an illuminated 'photo-mural' the size of a baseball pitch. The first suggestions that the ultimate air rights development might take the form of a tower sitting on top of the terminal itself and destroying all but the platform levels emerged in 1954. A 55-storey building was envisaged by Fellheimer and Wagner – ironically, the direct successors of Reed and Stem.[34] The developers William Zeckendorf and Roger Stevens, brought in by the New York Central, went further and proposed 80 storeys, with I M Pei as architect.[35] Warning bells began to sound in New York with the magazine *Architectural Forum,* under Douglas Haskell's editorship, launching a campaign to protect the building. In response, Alfred Fellheimer argued that 'neither pride nor reverence should be allowed to clot the vitality of a great metropolis'.[36]

For a few years, the proposals were left in abeyance, but they were forcefully revived in 1958 when the developer, Erwin Wolfson, commissioned Emery Roth to produce new designs for a massive tower. Roth, working with Walter Gropius and Pietro Belluschi,

37

38

37 The ramps linking the express and suburban concourses were later compromised by infilling to create office space.
38 Ticket booths in the 1930s: the notices advertise the great trains of the period, including a four-and-a-half-hour service to Boston.

39

40

23

41

designed the 59-storey block, later known as the PanAm Building, on the site of the former Railroad offices between the Terminal and the Grand Central Building.[37] Completed in 1963, the tower is one of the least happy post-war additions to the New York skyline, and a blot on the reputation of Gropius in particular, yet it was just part of a major rebuilding of the area around the Terminal which steadily replaced the apartment blocks and hotels of the earlier air rights development with a succession of corporate office slabs. Today, only one of the Park Avenue apartment blocks survives. Meanwhile, the Station itself reached its lowest ebb. Unbelievably, it was even proposed to insert a series of floors into the main waiting room to provide bowling alleys, while Westclox was allowed to suspend a vast and incongruous clock over the main concourse. Inappropriate shop fronts wrecked the harmony of the interior.

With Penn Station a lost cause – despite the efforts of campaigners such as Philip Johnson, Aline Saarinen, Peter Blake and Norval White – the fate of Grand Central mattered all the more. The Penn Station campaigners were all modernists – Johnson, for example, had worked with Mies van der Rohe on the Seagram Building, a few blocks up Park Avenue from Grand Central. Yet they came to question whether the classic Modern Movement urban formulae were right for Manhattan and came into con-

flict with distinguished architects of an older generation, like Walter Gropius and Marcel Breuer. The latter's plans for a further tower, squatting over the Terminal itself, were unveiled in 1967, though Breuer had produced ideas for rebuilding Grand Central as early as 1958. As high as the PanAm tower, the Breuer plans would have retained part of the main concourse and facade in its entirety but nothing else.

Grand Central was, in fact, designated a New York City Landmark in August, 1967. The New York City Landmarks Commission had come into being in 1965 and this was to be its first major battle. The Commission rejected Breuer's 800-foot tower as 'an architectural joke', declaring that Grand Central was 'one of the great buildings of America … a symbol of the city itself'.[38] When Breuer revised his design to retain all the concourse but remove parts of the facade, the Commission stood its ground and threw out the scheme.

Grand Central's owners were determined to fight the decision through the courts. Grand Central was, in fact, seen as one of the few serious assets of a failing business. The New York Central had merged with its old rival, the Pennsylvania Railroad, in 1968, but in 1972 the new Penn Central Railroad itself filed for bankruptcy. The legal battle continued until, in 1975, a judge in the Supreme Court of the State of New York ruled that the Landmarks Commission had acted wrongly and placed an 'economic hardship' on the collapsing Penn Central. The foundation of the Committee to Save Grand Central Terminal (with Jacqueline Onassis as a leading light) promised a rerun of the Penn Station campaign. This time, however, the outcome was very different. The court judgment was overturned on appeal later in 1975 and that judgment upheld in a further appeal process. Penn Central had only one avenue left – an appeal to the US Supreme Court. This was heard in 1978, after the Terminal had been designated a National Historic Landmark, and resulted, at last, in the final defeat of the development scheme – which had come to look like an historic relic. Preservation had become a serious force in the United States and landmark legislation was having a major impact on city planning. In New York, the victory of the campaign to save Grand Central was a turning point – no developer could thereafter afford to assume that the Landmark Commission was anything less than a formidable opponent. Many New Yorkers had come to realize (as Jacqueline Onassis put it) that 'New York City is the center of civilization in our day as Athens, Rome, Persepolis were in theirs'. [39]

The outcome of the long battle over the Terminal emerged as the private sector was passing out of the passenger rail business in New York. With Penn Central's railroad operations defunct, the running of the Terminal passed into the hands of a public body,

the Metropolitan Transit Authority and its subsidiary formed in 1983, Metro-North, who currently hold a long lease, but are likely to acquire the building outright in due course. Restoration work has been proceeding for a decade. A \$4.5 million renovation of the roof was completed in 1987. The vast Kodak sign was dismantled in 1990 and the east balcony reinstated. In 1991, a major restoration of the main waiting room began; the restored space is now used for exhibitions and social events. Work continues with the ceiling of the main concourse due to be completely restored. The total cost of the current restoration programme could top \$300 million – the price to be paid for decades of neglect.

Metro-North's masterplan for regenerating Grand Central is designed to provide New York with an efficient passenger station for the twenty-first century. More than 30,000 passengers still use the Terminal every day, but up to half a million people pass through the building daily; it is a massive interchange for subway passengers, a rendezvous, a tourist sight. As part of a typically American public/private development partnership, more restaurants and shops will be slotted into the building: it will become a destination for many who never see the interior of a commuter train. The space exists to provide for the diners and the shoppers, without turning Grand Central into the gaudy retail mart that Union Station,

42

43

44

42 The Terminal saw many famous faces. Here Coco Chanel departs in the *20th Century Limited* for Chicago.
43 Holiday crowds at the Terminal in July 1936.
44 The *20th Century Limited* departing at 6.00 pm for Chicago was the most famous of the luxury trains using Grand Central.

45 Grand in conception, the Terminal was also finely detailed using the best materials.
46 The detail over the gate to one of the suburban tracks.
47 Banks of elevators served the offices at upper levels.
48 The original track indicators, bearing the 'GCT' motif, remain in place.

45

46

47

48

Washington, has become. The main concourse is to remain inviolate – though restaurants and bars may colonise the long-deserted galleries. Philip Johnson has described Grand Central as the cathedral of New York.[40] Brushing aside St Patrick's and St John the Divine, he declares the Terminal to be the Notre Dame, the San Marco, of Manhattan – the spot where the spiritual energies of the city are experienced most forcibly. He is surely right. Grand Central is, perhaps, the one building that New York could not function without, the hub of Manhattan.

Grand Central has been widely characterised as a great public forum, a civic, more than a commercial, space. It is the product of an age where civic aspirations found a ready response amongst corporate developers. This fortuitous coincidence of interests survived into the 1930s, when the Rockefeller Center took up its multi-level circulation programme, installing a system of shops and restaurants, rather than trains, beneath a mass of office space.[41] The positive dynamic of Grand Central influenced progressive architects throughout the world. Sant'Elia, for example, took the inspiration for his multi-level station in the *Citta Nuova* from the Terminal.[42] Another radical architect, Le Corbusier, incorporated a rail terminal into his 1922 project for an ideal city – yet the station had become invisible, sunk below a huge pedestrian piazza surrounded by tall buildings.

So ingenious is the design of Grand Central that the trains themselves seem almost incidental. In this sense, the Terminal paved the way for the complete removal of the railroad from the surface of the city – the thinking which produced the generally-reviled rebuilding of Pennsylvania Station, but equally, the visionary project for a subterranean international station at London King's Cross by Norman Foster.

Indeed, Grand Central, with its clear sense of direction and careful management of the flow of people, offered a model for a distinctly twentieth century building type – the airport. In the second half of this century, airports have assumed the monumental character once unique to the great railroad stations. In turn, the new stations created by the rail revival of the 1980s and 90s have an expressive quality which has nothing to do with hiding the train away; they act as a necessary celebration of the survival and revival of rail travel. Grand Central is the product of a brief era when the railroads seemed to be the very lifeblood of the world's greatest city, the source of its commercial existence. The building, however, is inseparable from the massive programme of urban reconstruction of which it formed the centrepiece. Grand Central provides a model for the city which remains valid at the end of the twentieth century. As New York remakes itself as a metropolis for a new age, the continuing role of this great building is no longer in doubt.

Left Two New York icons: the massive dignity of Grand Central contrasts with the streamlined Art Deco styling of the 1930 Chrysler Building.

Right The MetLife (formerly PanAm) building now dominates views of the Terminal up Park Avenue. Grand Central was, however, saved from further mutilation by a spirited protest campaign.

Photographs

28

Above The Commodore Hotel has now been totally refaced in reflective glass – a bland neighbour for the Terminal and Chrysler Building.

Right The Terminal is treasured today as the expression of enlightened policies and of civic design.

Coutan's fine sculptural group, 'The Glory of Commerce', depicting the figures of Mercury, Minerva and Hercules, still dominates 42nd Street. The clock, installed in 1914, is over 13 feet high.

The architectural language of Grand Central is firmly classicist, though the style is used with restraint, even severity. The contrast between plain masonry and carved detail is central to the overall effect.

Recent restoration work –
still proceeding – has
reinstated much of the
splendour of the main
concourse. The clock on
the main concourse is a
familiar meeting place for
travellers.

The original ticket booths remain in position, though now altered and surmounted by a modern indicator board.

Cleaning has revealed the original details which are executed in cast stone of very high quality.

LOW

Left Light pours into the suburban concourse from the large windows.
Right Recent improvements have included the opening of a cafe at gallery level.

Left The recent restoration of the main (express) waiting room has opened it up as a space for exhibitions and other events.

Left, above, right The fine details of the room have been carefully conserved, though passengers today no longer wait on the wooden benches.

Left and above The huge light fittings of the waiting room have been carefully cleaned and rewired.
Right The MetLife Building makes an impact on the main concourse, its banks of escalators ruthlessly – if effectively – cutting into the original space.

ENTRANCE TO
TRACK·110   TRACK·109

Left Years of under-investment had some positive consequences. Original details like these track indicators remained untouched.

Above The ramp system continues down to track level; it was to be emulated in many later developments.

Right Original light fittings survived intact through years of neglect and have now been restored.

Far right The suburban concourse today contains few facilities. Plans for the restoration of the Terminal would locate new uses here, leaving the main concourse unchanged.

Far left Walkways behind the great windows of the main concourse – floored in glass to allow maximum light penetration – provide access to upper-level offices.

Left and above The roof of the building is supported on a great mass of concealed structural steelwork.

Above left The great windows feature the original mechanisms, which allowed for natural ventilation.

Above Details, such as the stair balustrades, are firmly rooted in a Beaux-Arts tradition.

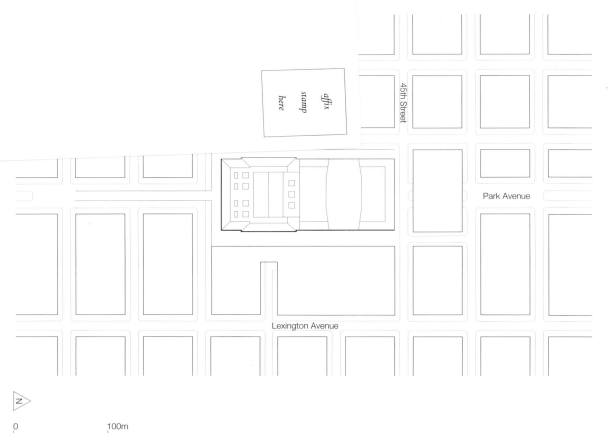

PHAIDON PRESS LIMITED
Customer Service Department
Regent's Wharf
All Saints Street
London N1 9PA
England

*affix
stamp
here*

45th Street

Park Avenue

Lexington Avenue

N

0   100m

0   300ft

Floor plans

1 concourse
2 platforms
3 lower concourse
4 waiting room
5 restaurant
6 tea room
7 ramp to street
8 main station building
9 Terminal Building driveway
10 incoming baggage
11 outgoing baggage
12 Post Office building
13 Biltmore Hotel
14 The Roosevelt

50

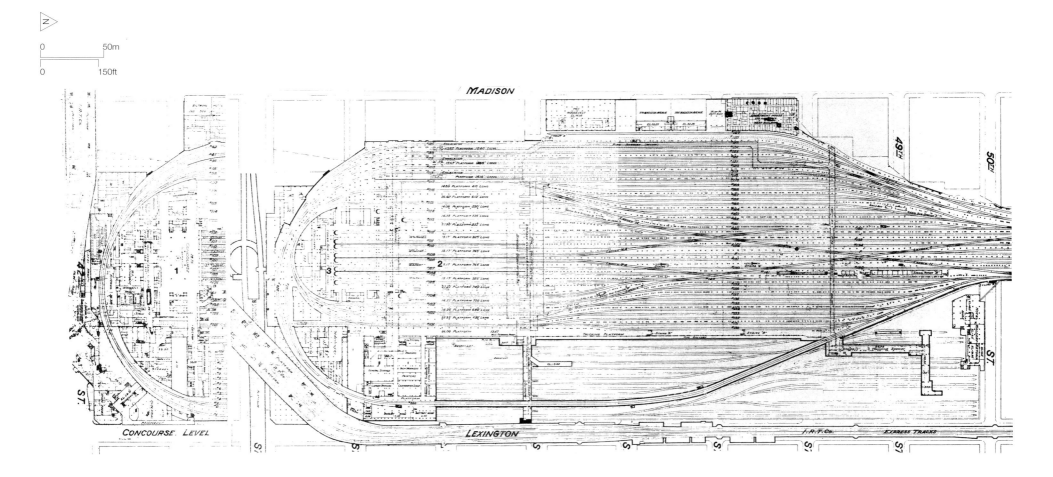

Suburban level

*All drawings on pages 50–51 are
dated 1931, revised 1952*

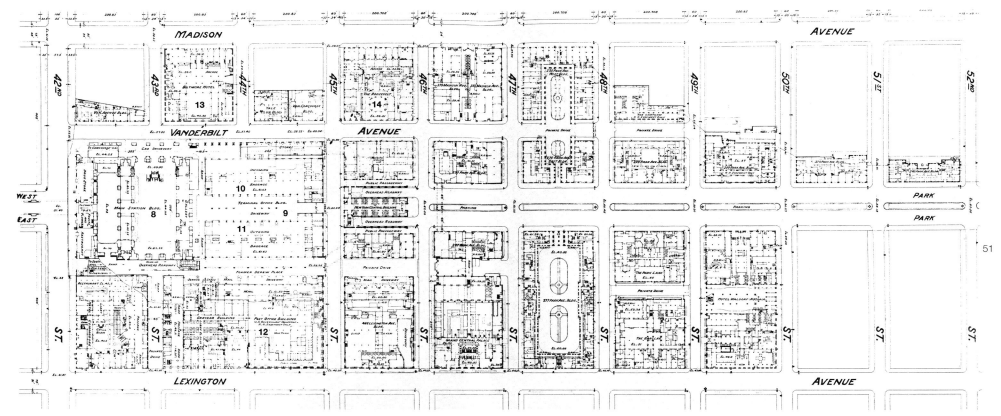

Street level

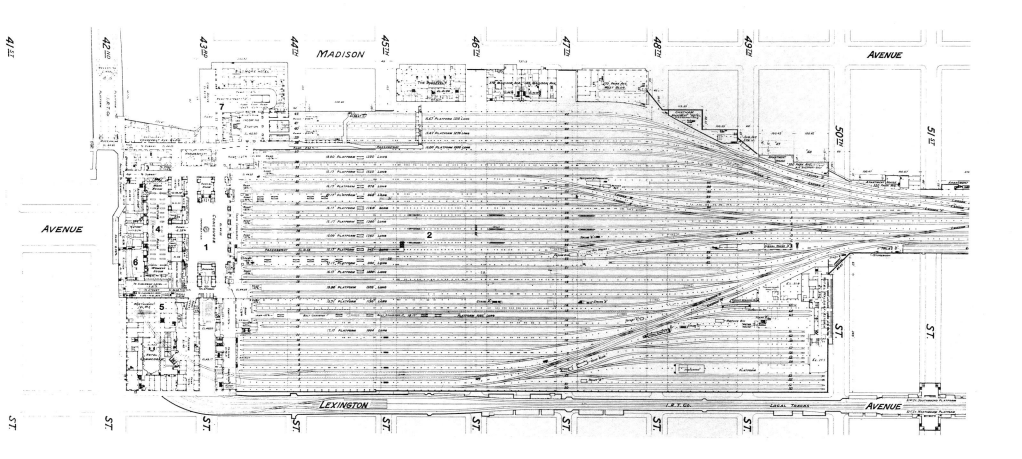

Express level

Vanderbilt Avenue

East 42nd Street

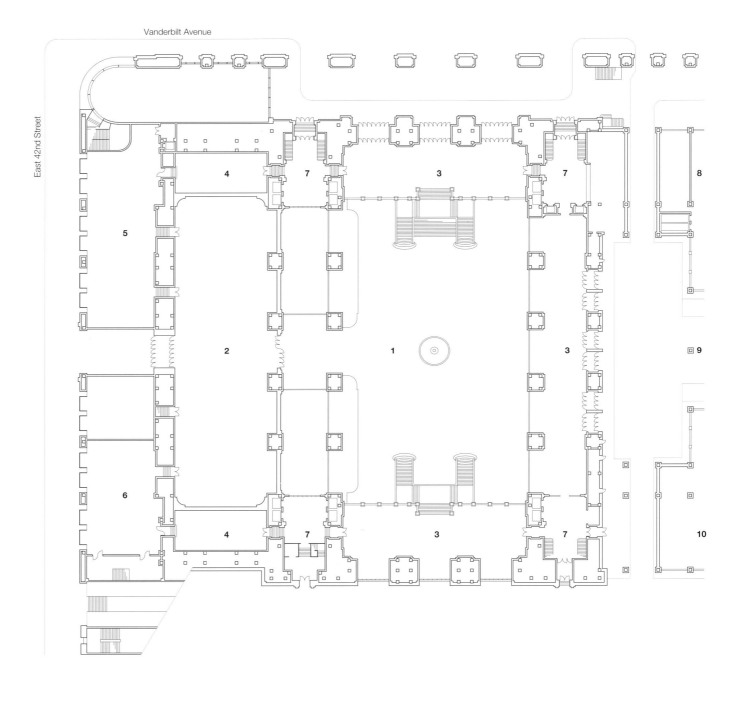

4

7

3

7

8

5

2

1

3

9

6

4

7

3

7

10

N

0   20m

0   60ft

Street level

Drawing on this page is dated 1911; those on
page 53 are dated 1989

Floor plans

1 concourse
2 waiting room
3 gallery
4 office
5 stores
6 restaurant
7 entrance hall
8 incoming baggage
9 cab drive
10 outgoing baggage
11 express concourse
   below
12 waiting room below
13 library
14 offices
15 tennis courts
16 lounge
17 weight room
18 massage room
19 men's lockers
20 women's lockers

53

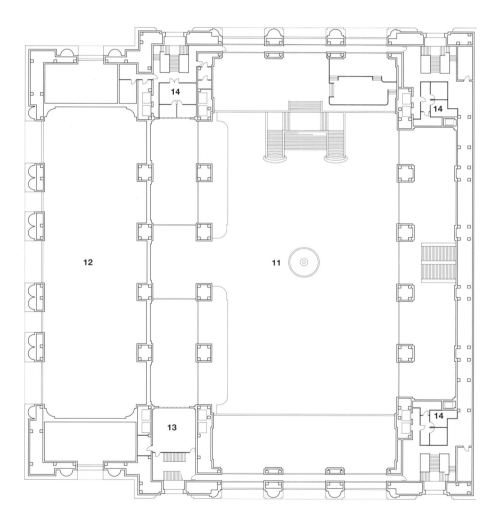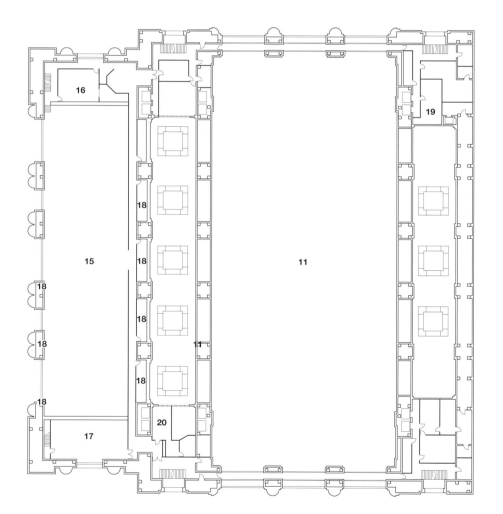

First floor and third floor level

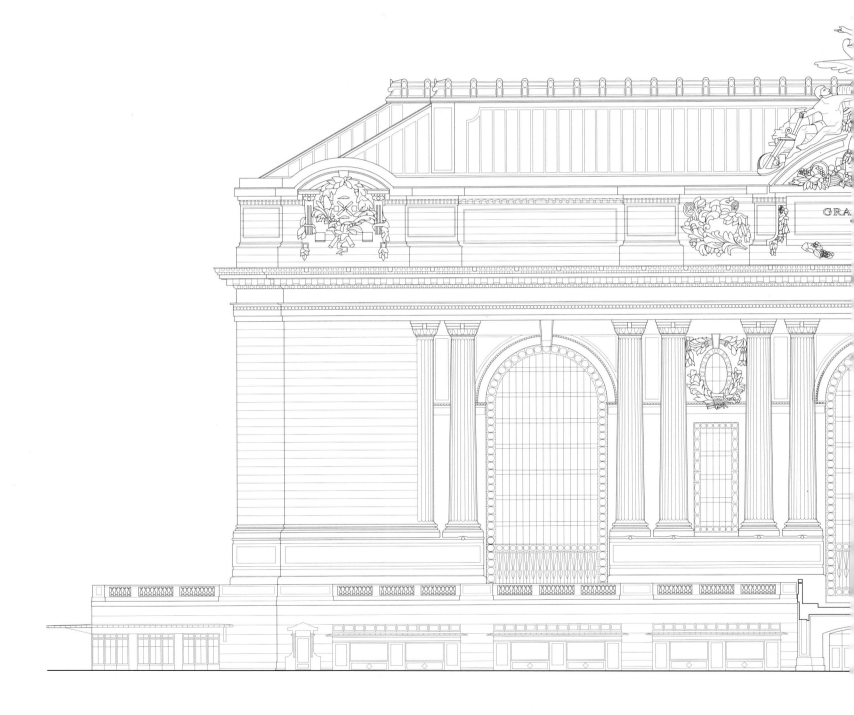

0   5m

0   15ft

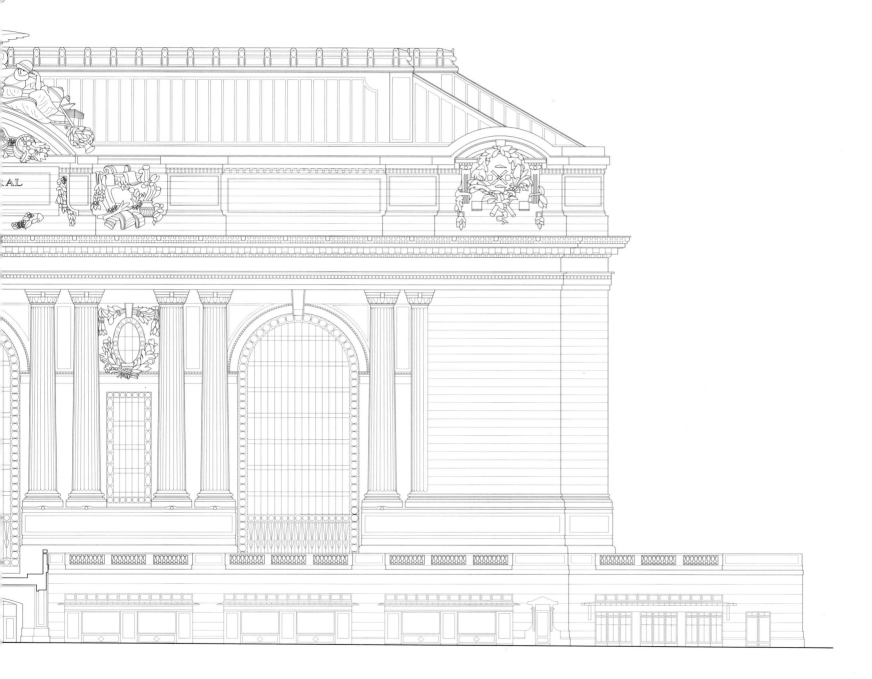

Elevation shows Coutan's sculpture 'The Glory of Commerce', 1914

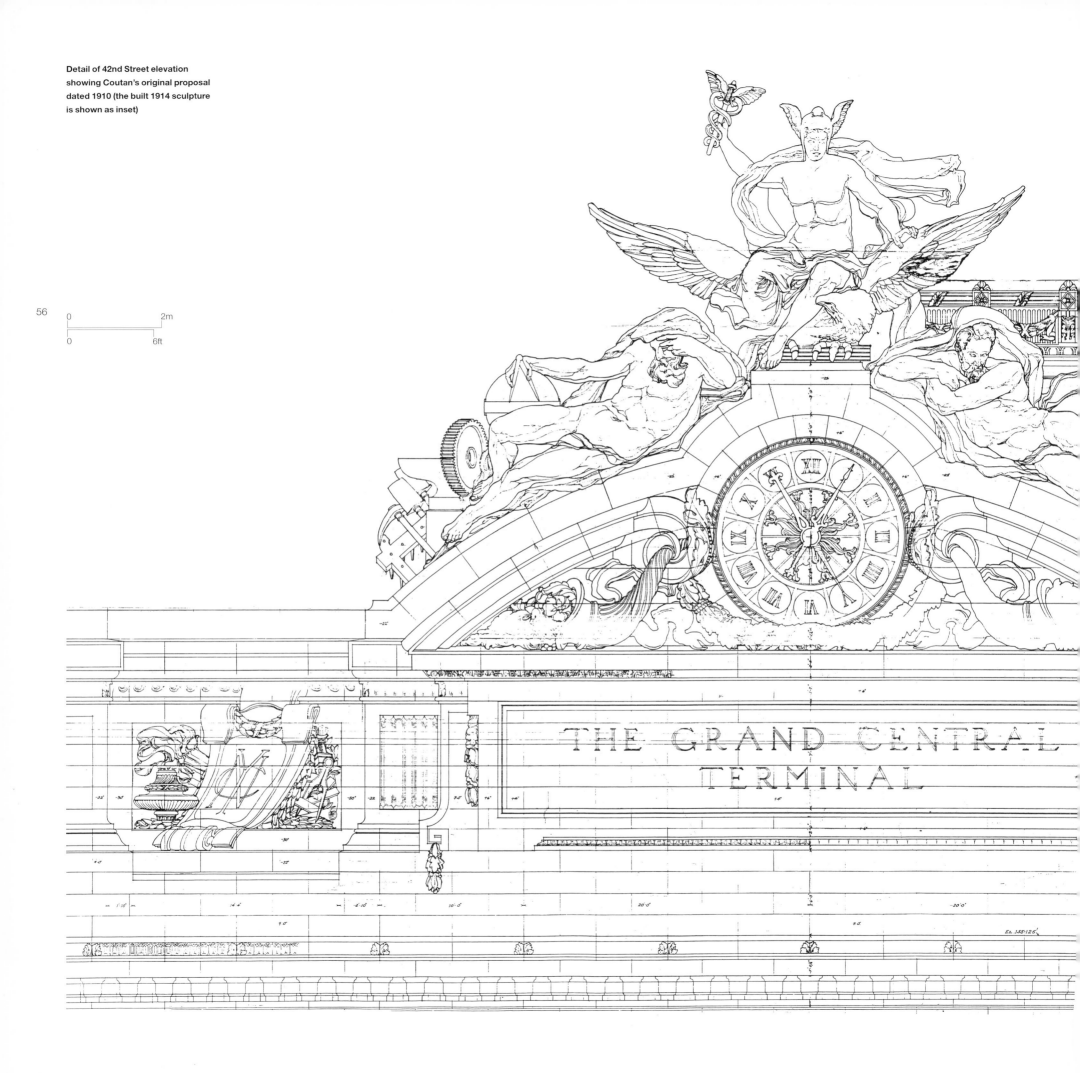

Detail of 42nd Street elevation
showing Coutan's original proposal
dated 1910 (the built 1914 sculpture
is shown as inset)

56

THE GRAND CENTRAL
TERMINAL

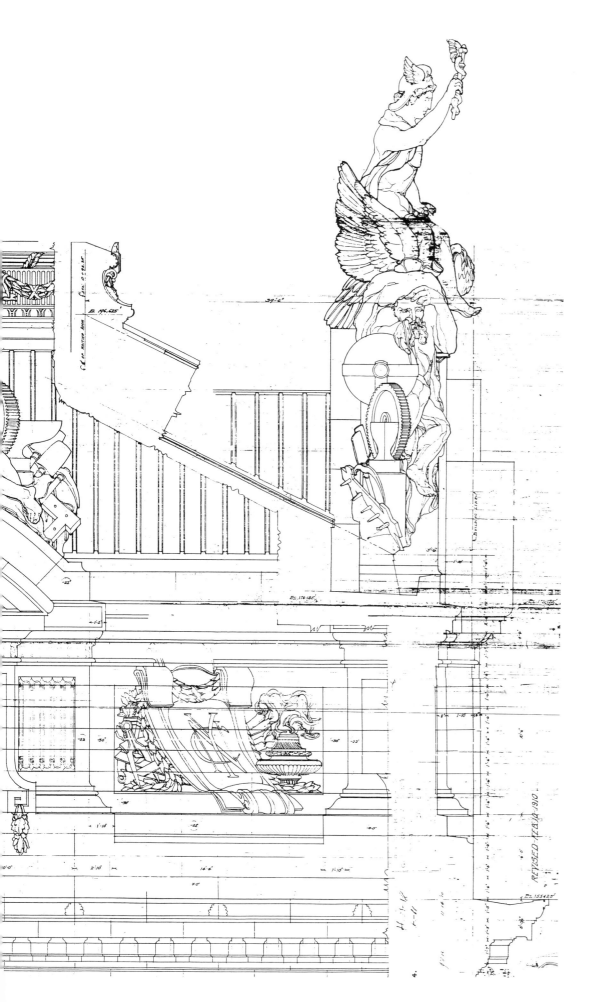

GRAND CENTRAL
TERMINAL

Cross section through
43rd Street looking north

1 concourse
2 information
3 art gallery
4 art school
5 Grand Central Theatre
6 express loop
7 suburban outer loop
8 suburban inner loop
9 platforms
10 battery room
11 rotary room
12 cab drive

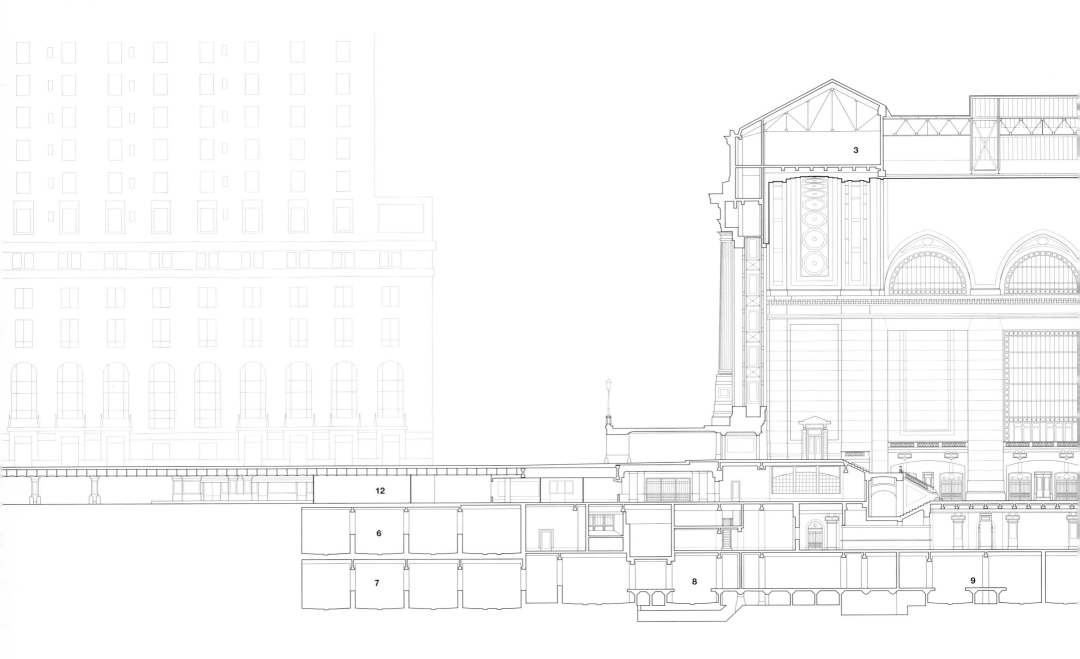

0   10m

0   30ft

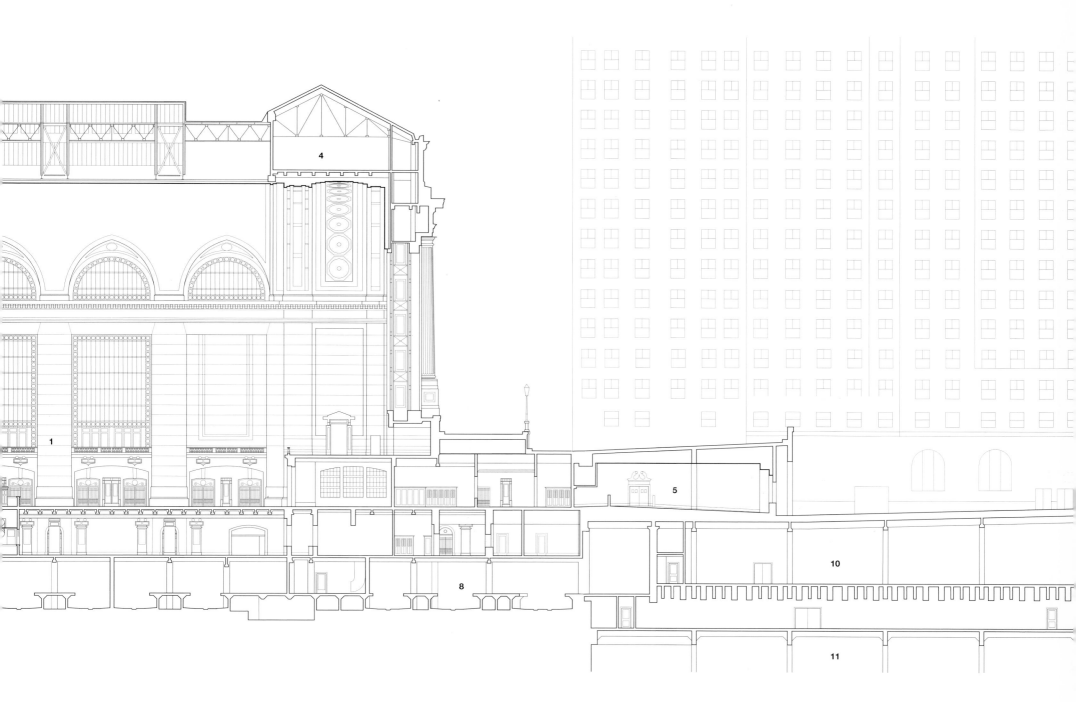

Based on drawing dated 1916

Author's acknowledgements

I would like to thank Metro-North Railroad for allowing me access to every part of Grand Central and to its records. Wayne Ehmann, Chief Architect to Metro-North, was generous of his time and advice. Thanks are also due to Dan Brucker of the Metro-North press office and to Manny Patel, for producing material from the archive of drawings still held at the Terminal.

The other principal unpublished sources are the William J Wilgus Papers in the Manuscripts Department of the New York Public Library and the Warren and Wetmore Collection held in the Avery Library of Columbia University. My thanks are due to the staff of both institutions.

I also acknowledge the excellent historical report produced for Metro-North by Deborah Rau and Jim Rhodes of Beyer Blinder Belle as part of the Grand Central Terminal Master Plan.

Illustration acknowledgements

Illustrations are provided courtesy of: Avery Library, Columbia University: fig 35; Metro-North Commuter Railroad: figs 5, 9, 11, 13, 15, 23, 27, 30–33, 37–42, 44–46 (figs 45 and 46 by Frank English); Range: figs 1–4, 6, 12, 24, 29, 43.

Notes

1 Vincent Scully, *American Architecture and Urbanism* (New York, 1969).
2 Nathan Silver, *Lost New York* (Boston, 1967), pp37–8.
3 *New York Times*, 2 February, 1913.
4 For the early history of the New York & Harlem, see Louis V Grogan, *The Coming of the New York & Harlem Railroad* (Pawling, NY, 1989). For accounts of the early railways in New York, see Carl W Condit, *The Port of New York: A History of the Rail and Terminal System from the Beginnings to Pennsylvania Station* (Chicago, 1980) (the first part of a magisterial account), and Alvin F Harlow, *The Road of the Century: the Story of the New York Central* (New York, 1947).
5 For Cornelius Vanderbilt's role in the New York Central, see Condit, *op cit*.
6 Robert A M Stern, G Gilmartin and J Massengale, *New York 1900* (New York, 1983), p307 *et ff*.
7 For Snook, see Margot Gayle and Edmund V Gillon Jnr, *Cast Iron in New York* (Toronto, 1974).
8 *Ibid*.
9 James Marston Fitch and Diana S Waite, *Grand Central Terminal and Rockefeller Center: A Historic-Critical Estimate of their Significance* (New York, 1971), contains a good summary of the history of Grand Central I.
10 W J Wilgus, 'The Grand Central Terminal in Perspective' (1939), typescript in Wilgus Papers, NYPL.
11 *Ibid*.
12 *Ibid*.
13 For a detailed illustrated account of the rebuilding process see *Inception and Creation of the Grand Central Terminal*, privately printed for Stem and Fellheimer, 1913. Copy in Wilgus Papers, NYPL. See also Wilgus Papers, Box 17 – a collection of construction photographs.
14 Stern *et al*, *op cit*.
15 Leland M Roth, *McKim, Mead & White, Architects* (London, 1984), p183.
16 All the schemes which survive are illustrated in Deborah Nevins *et al*, *Grand Central Terminal: City Within the City* (New York, 1982), pp12–13. See also Carl W Condit, *The Port of New York: A History of the Rail and Terminal System from the Grand Central Electrification to the Present* (Chicago, 1981), pp63–5. The perspectives by McKim, Mead and White are preserved in the archives of the New York Historical Society.
17 Wilgus, *op cit*.
18 Stern, *op cit*; D Nevins, *op cit*, p142; biographical notes in Warren and Wetmore Collection, Avery Library, Columbia University.
19 Wilgus, *op cit*.
20 Condit, *op cit* (1981), p69.
21 Wilgus's later projects include a tunnel under the Detroit River and work for the US War Department. He died at Claremont, New Hampshire, in 1949.
22 Wilgus Papers, NYPL, undated cutting.
23 See Condit, *op cit* (1981), pp54–100 for a detailed account of the construction process.
24 Nevins, *op cit*, pp16,18. Jules-Alexis Coutan's most famous work was the huge carving of 'Armed France' on the Alexander III bridge in Paris. The Grand Central Terminal sculpture was made by Wm Bradley & Sons of Long Island City. It took six weeks to assemble on the site. Coutan seems never to have visited the USA and expressed a dislike for its architecture and art. He was clearly recruited by Whitney Warren, whose links with France remained close. (Information on Coutan from Dr Ed Diestelkamp.)
25 Harlow, *op cit*.
26 Nevins, *op cit*, pp16,18.
27 Information from Mr Wayne Ehmann.
28 A perspective of this proposal is in the Warren and Wetmore Collection at the Avery Library.
29 Carroll L V Meeks, *The Railroad Station: An Architectural History* (New Haven, 1956), p130.
30 The technique was invented by a Catalan, Raphael Guastavino, and used by McKim, Mead and White at the Boston Public Library c1889. See Leland M Roth, *op cit*, pp124–5.
31 Condit, *op cit* (1981), p77.
32 *Ibid*, p95.
33 Wilgus, *op cit*.
34 Fellheimer and Wagner's masterpiece was Union Station, Cincinnatti, built in 1929–33. They were also responsible for Central Station, Buffalo, NY, and North Station, Boston.
35 For Pei's involvement with William Zeckendorf see Carter Wiseman, *The Architecture of I M Pei* (London, 1990), pp47–71.
36 Condit, *op cit* (1981), p242.
37 Elliott Wilensky and Norval White, *AIA Guide to New York City* (3rd edn, New York, 1988), p244. For a (not very convincing) defence of Gropius's role, see Henry Isaacs, *Gropius: An Illustrated Biography of the Creator of the Bauhaus* (1990), pp283–4.
38 Condit, *op cit*, p250.
39 Foreword to Nevins, *op cit*.
40 Philip Johnson's programme on Grand Central in the BBC TV series, 'Building Sights America' was broadcast in Britain in 1993.
41 Fitch and Waite, *op cit*; Carol H Krinsky, *Rockefeller Center* (New York, 1978).
42 The Grand Central plans were published in *Italiana* (Milan) in 1913. See Douglas Haskell, 'Futurism with its covers on', *Architectural Review*, May 1975, pp301–4.

Select bibliography of principal published sources

Condit Carl W, *The Port of New York* (2 vols, Chicago, 1980, 1981).
Fitch James Marston and Diana S Waite, *Grand Central Terminal and Rockefeller Center: A Historic-Critical Estimate of their Significance* (New York, 1971). *The Gateway to a Continent* (New York, nd ?1939).
Harlow Alvin F, *The Road of the Century: The Story of the New York Central* (New York, 1947).
Marshall David, *Grand Central* (New York/London, 1946).
Meeks Carroll L V, *The Railroad Station: An Architectural History* (New Haven, 1956).
Middleton William D, *Grand Central, The World's Greatest Railway Terminal* (San Marino, USA, 1977).
Nevins Deborah *et al*, *Grand Central Terminal, City Within the City* (New York, 1982).
Scully Vincent, *American Architecture and Urbanism* (New York, 1969).
Silver Nathan, *Lost New York* (Boston, 1967).
Stern Robert A M *et al*, *New York 1900* (New York, 1983).

Chronology

1871 Opening of the first Grand Central Terminal.
1897–8 External reconstruction of Grand Central I.
1899 Appointment of William J Wilgus as Chief Engineer to New York Central Railroad.
1900 Internal refurbishment of Terminal.
1901 Publication of Wilgus's plans for two-level terminus.
1902 Fatal accident leads to decision to electrify lines into Grand Central.
1903 Limited competition for design of new Terminal – won by Reed and Stem. Beginning of construction work.
1904 Appointment of Warren and Wetmore, who join Reed and Stem in Associated Architects of Grand Central Terminal. New designs produced.
1907 Resignation of William Wilgus from NYCRR.
1908 Old train shed demolished.
1910 Demolition of remainder of Grand Central I.
1911 Construction work begins on new Terminal. Death of Charles Reed and appointment of Warren and Wetmore as sole architects.
1912 Partial opening of new Terminal.
1913 Official opening of new Terminal (1 February).
1914 Opening of Biltmore Hotel.
1927 Graybar Building completed.
1930 Completion of New York Central (Helmsley) Building.
1931 Waldorf-Astoria Hotel opens.
1947 Record 250,000 passengers use the Terminal in one day.
1954 Designs for office tower on top of Terminal unveiled. Protest campaign.
1958 Plans for PanAm Building published (completed 1963).
1967 Grand Central designated a New York City Landmark.
1968 Merger of New York Central and Pennsylvania Railroads to form Penn Central. 800 foot tower proposed for Grand Central by Marcel Breuer: rejected by Landmarks Commission.
1975 Landmark designation quashed in New York State Supreme Court, but Grand Central subsequently added to National Register of Historic Places.
1976 Grand Central becomes National Historic Landmark.
1978 US Supreme Court upholds Landmark status of Grand Central.
1987 Renovation of main roof of Terminal.
1988 Publication of Grand Central Terminal Master Plan.
1990 Removal of Kodak sign from east balcony.
1991–3 Refurbishment of waiting room.
1994 Restoration of concourse ceiling begins.